West's Federal Taxation

 S0-DON-752

SUMMARY OF IRS RESTRUCTURING AND REFORM ACT OF 1998

William H. Hoffman, Jr.
J.D., Ph.D., C.P.A., *University of Houston*

Eugene Willis
Ph.D., C.P.A., *University of Illinois at Urbana*

James E. Smith
Ph.D., C.P.A., *College of William and Mary*

William A. Raabe
Ph.D., C.P.A., *Samford University*

David M. Maloney
Ph.D., C.P.A., *University of Virginia*

Jon S. Davis
Ph.D., C.P.A., *University of Illinois at Urbana*

Wayne H. Shaw
Ph.D., C.P.A., *Southern Methodist University*

Prepared by
Raymond Wacker
Ph.D., C.P.A., *Southern Illinois University at Carbondale*

West/South-Western College Publishing
an International Thomson Publishing company I(T)P®

Cincinnati • Albany • Boston • Detroit • Johannesburg • London • Madrid • Melbourne • Mexico City
New York • Pacific Grove • San Francisco • Scottsdale • Singapore • Tokyo • Toronto

Accounting Team Director: Richard K. Lindgren
Acquisitions Editor: Alex von Rosenberg
Developmental Editor: Esther Craig
Production Editor: Rebecca Glaab
Marketing Manager: Maureen Riopelle
Manufacturing Coordinator: Gordon Woodside

ISBN: 0-324-01306-X

1 2 3 4 5 6 7   WST   4 3 2 1 0 9 8

Printed in the United States of America

International Thomson Publishing
WEST/South-Western College Publishing is an ITP Company.
The ITP trademark is used under license.

INTRODUCTION

On July 22, 1998 the Internal Revenue Service Restructuring and Reform Act of 1998 (hereinafter Act) was signed into law. This Act restructured the IRS in response to highly publicized Senate Finance Committee hearings regarding long-standing administrative abuses on the part of the IRS. These hearings characterized the IRS as a bureaucracy that was highly centralized, rigid, and out of control. Worse, the Service was also seen as a tax collector often unconcerned with the equity of its procedures or the consequences that its actions had on the lives of taxpayers. In reorganizing the IRS, Congress intended to create a "kinder and gentler" IRS. Whether or not that hope will be fulfilled, it is certain that the IRS will be far more restricted in carrying out its operations.

This summary discusses the salient features of the new law as they relate to topical coverage contained within the textbooks comprising the West's Federal Taxation Series published by WEST/South-Western College Publishing. Provisions of the Act which directly relate to any textbook within this series listed below are summarized within this supplement. In each instance, provisions discussed have been cross-referenced with the applicable textbook and with the appropriate section of the Internal Revenue Code. Given widespread public interest in the new law as well as the sheer depth of IRS restructuring, issues not within the scope of West's Federal Taxation Series textbooks are also included as they may be of interest to professors and students enrolled in courses normally using such texts. Professors and students alike must realize that the Act is quite extensive and highly technical so that the vast majority of its provisions are of interest only in courses limited to IRS procedures.

The Internal Revenue Service Restructuring and Reform Act of 1998 also contains tax provisions not related to the restructuring of the IRS. Additionally, it contains the Tax Technical Corrections Act of 1998, which corrects numerous technical errors found in the Taxpayer Relief Act of 1997 and previous tax legislation. These additional provisions comprise the second part of this supplement. Provisions discussed have again been cross-referenced with the applicable textbook and with the appropriate section of the Internal Revenue Code. Only those provisions within the scope of the textbooks in the West's Federal Taxation Series will be discussed.

This supplement is specifically intended to accompany the following texts:

Hoffman, Smith, and Willis, *West's Federal Taxation: Individual Income Taxes: 1999 Edition*, (hereinafter INDIVIDUAL TEXT).

Hoffman, Raabe, Smith, and Maloney, *West's Federal Taxation: Corporations, Partnerships, Estates, and Trusts: 1999 Edition*, (hereinafter CORPORATIONS TEXT).

Willis, Hoffman, Maloney, and Raabe, *West's Federal Taxation: Comprehensive Volume: 1999 Edition*, (hereinafter COMPREHENSIVE TEXT).

Willis and Davis, *West's Federal Taxation: An Introduction to Business Entities: 1999 Edition*, (hereinafter BUSINESS ENTITIES TEXT).

Davis and Shaw, *West's Federal Taxation: Advanced Taxation: 1999 Edition*, (hereinafter ADVANCED TEXT).

Smith, *West's Internal Revenue Code of 1986 and Treasury Regulations: Annotated and Selected: 1999 Edition*, (hereinafter CODE & REGS). Note: The applicable sections of this title have been cross-referenced with the relevant pages of this supplement in an appendix found on the last page of this supplement.

One final word of caution. Readers must be advised that changes relating to the taxation of capital gains and losses are extensive and can only be highlighted in this supplement. Since the effects of these changes are far-reaching, pages 3-27 through 3-29 of Chapter 3 of the INDIVIDUAL TEXT and all of Chapter 16 of the INDIVIDUAL TEXT have been rewritten. Both are currently available on the WEST/South-Western College Publishing website at tax.swcollege.com. Please read the changes in both chapters for a thorough understanding of the new capital gain and loss rules.

TABLE OF CONTENTS

TOPIC	PAGE

PART 1: IRS RESTRUCTURING AND REORGANIZATION

REORGANIZATION OF THE IRS

The most far-reaching effect of the Act lies in its fundamental overhauling of the organizational structure and governance of the IRS. The apparent intent behind this legislation is to transform a rigid and insensitive bureaucracy into a customer service-oriented agency.

IRS Mission Statement and Organizational Structure

As with prior law, the IRS Commissioner possesses wide latitude in establishing the mission statement and organizational structure of the IRS. The new law directs the Commissioner to revise the IRS's mission statement to provide greater emphasis on serving the public and meeting the needs of taxpayers. The Commissioner is also directed to restructure the IRS by eliminating or substantially modifying the current three-tier geographical structure (national, regional, and district) and replacing it with an organizational structure based on operational units serving particular groups of taxpayers with similar needs.

EFFECTIVE DATE - July 22, 1998. Revised organizational structure plan is due by January 18, 1999.

CORPORATIONS TEXT - pp. 16-4 and 16-5.
ADVANCED TEXT - pp. 14-4 and 5.

IRS Officers and Personnel

The duties of the IRS Commissioner remain similar as under prior law. The qualifications for appointment now include demonstrated ability in management. The IRS Commissioner will now serve a five year term beginning on the date of appointment and may be reappointed to subsequent terms.

The duties of the IRS Chief Counsel are also largely unchanged except that he is no longer an Assistant General Counsel of the Treasury but instead reports directly to the IRS Commissioner. An independent Treasury Inspector General for Tax Administration replaces the IRS Office of the Chief Inspector. All powers and duties except for certain personnel matters are transferred to the former.

The Act also requires the IRS to make greater use of personnel flexibilities providing this does not violate existing merit system principles, prohibited personnel practices, preference eligibles and negotiated union rules. The Act also revises the IRS's performance management system and rules governing mandatory termination for misconduct.

EFFECTIVE DATE - July 22, 1998, except that the Office of Treasury Inspector General for Tax Administrative is not effective until January 18, 1999.

CORPORATIONS TEXT - p. 16-5.
ADVANCED TEXT - pp. 14-4 and 14-5.

IRC § REFERENCE - §§7803 and 7804.

Congressional Oversight

Not surprisingly, Congressional action to correct bureaucratic misconduct mandates multiple notifications to Congress. The IRS Commissioner and the IRS Oversight Board discussed below are required to submit reports dealing with diverse matters such as tax law complexity, budgeting issues, and data gathering to Congress. In addition, annual reports dealing with tax law application, taxpayer compliance and errors commonly encountered by taxpayers, confidentiality of taxpayer information, IRS Revenue Officers' interpretation of tax law, and areas of ambiguity must be made to the House Ways and Means Committee and the Senate Finance Committee.

EFFECTIVE DATE - July 22, 1998, except that specified reports to Congress are due on different dates.

IRS Oversight Board

The Act establishes a new IRS Oversight Board within the Department of the Treasury. Although only advisory, this Board is empowered to inspect and evaluate all aspects of the administration, management, conduct, direction and supervision of the IRS. Under the Act, the Board has five general responsibilities:

1.   Develop strategic plans for the IRS.
2.   Review the IRS's operational strategies.
3.   Render appropriate management recommendations.
4.   Review the IRS's budget.
5.   Ensure proper treatment of taxpayers by IRS employees.

While this Board is authorized to oversee general law enforcement matters and has the responsibility to ensure that the organization and operation of the IRS allows the IRS to carry out its mission, it has no authority to develop or recommend Federal tax policy nor may it intervene in either specific taxpayer cases or specific personnel matters.

The IRS Oversight Board will consist of nine members. The first thee members are the Secretary of the Treasury (or the Deputy Secretary), the IRS Commissioner and a full-time Federal employee, probably from the IRS. The remaining six members are private citizens. These members are to be selected based on their expertise in management of large service organizations, customer service, Federal tax law, information technology, organizational development, and the needs and concerns of taxpayers and small business.

EFFECTIVE DATE - July 22, 1998. The six private citizens are to be appointed by the President and confirmed by the Senate by January 18, 1999.

IRC § REFERENCE - §7802.

National Taxpayer Advocacy

The Act replaces the IRS Taxpayer Advocate with the National Taxpayer Advocate. This new advocate is independent in authority and possess a wide range of powers in order to address problems encountered by groups of taxpayers. The National Taxpayer Advocate will also direct a system of local Taxpayer Advocates who comprise the primary resolution system and operate independently from the IRS's examination, collection, and appeals functions.

The Act also expands the circumstances under which a Taxpayer Assistance Order may be issued if a taxpayer is suffering from a significant hardship.

EFFECTIVE DATE - July 22, 1998.

CORPORATIONS TEXT - Figure 16-1 on p. 16-4.
ADVANCED TEXT - Figure 14-1 on p. 14-4.

IRC § REFERENCE - §7803(c).

COURT JURISDICTION

The jurisdictional and procedural changes affecting the U.S. Tax Court include the following:

1.   Cases over which the Small Cases Division of the U.S. Tax Court has jurisdiction have been increased from $10,000 to $50,000.

2.   The U.S. Tax Court has sole jurisdiction with respect to disputes concerning innocent spouse relief discussed below.

3.   The U.S. Tax Court has jurisdiction over an adverse IRS Appeals decision in the case of an administrative protest of a proposed IRS levy.

4.   Any tax deficiency notice sent by the IRS must advise the taxpayer of the last day he can file a case with the U.S. Tax Court.

5.   The U.S. Tax Court can order a refund of any tax collected during a period the IRS was prohibited from assessing or collecting a tax deficiency and can order a refund of any overpayment not appealed by the IRS.

The U.S. Court of Federal Claims and the U.S. District Courts also have jurisdiction to determine the correct amount of estate tax liability in actions brought by estates consisting primarily of closely-held businesses.

EFFECTIVE DATE - July 22, 1998.

INDIVIDUAL TEXT - pp. 2-13 and 2-14.
CORPORATIONS TEXT - pp. 1-25 through 1-27.
COMPREHENSIVE TEXT - pp. 28-12 through 28-14.
BUSINESS ENTITIES TEXT - pp. 2-12 and 2-13.
CODE & REGS - §7463.

IRC § REFERENCE - §§6212, 6213, 7422, and 7463.

STATUTE OF LIMITATIONS, INTEREST, AND PENALTIES

Statute of Limitations

The Act allows for the suspension of the statute of limitations for refund claims for any time period during which a taxpayer is unable to manage his financial affairs due to a medically determinable physical or mental impairment that can be expected to result in death or last for a continuous period of not less than 12 months. The statute of limitations is not suspended if the taxpayer's spouse or another person is authorized to act on the taxpayer's behalf in financial matters. This provision represents a reversal of the Supreme Court's 1977 ruling in *U.S. v. Brockamp*.

EFFECTIVE DATE - Periods of disability before, on, or after July 22, 1998 but does not apply to any claim for refund or credit that is barred by the statute of limitations as of July 22, 1998.

INDIVIDUAL TEXT - pp. 1-20 and 1-21.
CORPORATIONS TEXT - pp. 16-22 through 16-24.
COMPREHENSIVE TEXT - pp. 25-20 and 25-21.
ADVANCED TEXT - pp. 14-24 through 14-26.

IRC § REFERENCE - §6511(h).

IRS Penalties

The Act makes several changes regarding penalties on tax underpayments. Examples include the following:

1.   The penalty for failure to pay taxes is lowered from .50 percent per month to .25 percent per month in the case of an individual who filed a timely return and has an installment payment agreement with the IRS in effect. The maximum ceiling of 25 percent still applies.

2.   In the case of the penalty for failure to make deposits, the taxpayer can now designate the period to which each deposit is to be applied. This designation must be made no later than 90 days after the date of the IRS penalty notice. This provision should alleviate the harshness of the FIFO system used by the IRS in accounting for tax deposits.

3.   The accrual of certain penalties is suspended after one year if the IRS fails to send the taxpayer a notice specifically stating the taxpayer's liability for additional taxes. This suspension is available only to an individual taxpayer whose tax return was timely filed. Nor does it apply to an individual taxpayer who either filed a fraudulent tax return or who has been assessed criminal penalties.

4.   In order for the IRS to assess any penalty, the notice of deficiency must state the name of the penalty, the Code section involved, and a computation of the penalty.

EFFECTIVE DATE - Generally, taxable years ending after July 22, 1998.

INDIVIDUAL TEXT - pp. 1-21 and 1-22.
CORPORATIONS TEXT - pp. 16-15 through 16-17.
COMPREHENSIVE TEXT - pp. 25-13 through 25-15.
ADVANCED TEXT - pp. 14-18 through 14-24.

IRC § REFERENCE - §§6404, 6651, and 6751.

Taxpayer Interest Payments

The Act also makes various changes regarding taxpayer interest payments on tax underpayments. Examples include the following:

1.   The new law allows for interest netting in cases where interest charged or accrued on tax overpayments and underpayments involving the same taxpayer are equivalent. In this case, the interest charged will be zero. The interest netting rules cover any tax imposed by the Internal Revenue Code.

2.   The overpayment interest rate will be AFR plus three percentage points, except for corporations whose rate is AFR plus two percentage points.

3.   The Act also provides that taxpayers located within a Presidentially declared disaster area do not have to pay interest on taxes due for the length of any extension for filing their returns granted by the Secretary of the Treasury.

4.   As is the case with penalties, the accrual of interest after one year is suspended if the IRS fails to send the taxpayer a notice specifically stating the taxpayer's liability for additional taxes. This suspension applies solely to an individual taxpayer filing a timely nonfraudulent return and who does not face criminal penalties during the time of interest suspension.

5.   Every IRS notice that includes an amount of interest required to be paid by an individual taxpayer must state the Code section involved and a detailed computation of the interest.

EFFECTIVE DATE - Generally, taxable years ending after July 22, 1998.

INDIVIDUAL TEXT - pp. 1-21 and 1-22.
CORPORATIONS TEXT - pp. 16-13 through 16-15.
COMPREHENSIVE TEXT - pp. 25-11 through 25-13.
ADVANCED TEXT - pp. 14-16 and 14-17.

IRC § REFERENCE - §§6404 and 6621.

TAYPAYER PROTECTION DURING IRS AUDIT OR COLLECTION ACTIVITIES

Burden of Proof

The Act provides that the IRS has the burden of proof in all court proceedings with respect to any factual issue if the taxpayer introduces credible evidence with respect to any factual issue relevant to ascertaining the taxpayer's tax liability. This shifting of the burden of proof is not complete in that the following four restrictions apply.

1. The taxpayer must still substantiate any tax benefit claimed. This requirement is identical to prior law.

2. The taxpayer must maintain records required under prior tax law.

3. The taxpayer must cooperate with reasonable requests made by the IRS for meetings, interviews, witnesses, information, and documents.

4. In the case of nonindividual taxpayers, the shifting of the burden of proof is not available to taxpayers who possess a net worth of more than $7 million or who employ more than 500 persons. Both requirements are identical to existing limitations governing the awarding of attorney's fees. This restriction applies to income, estate, gift, and generation-skipping transfer taxes.

The Act shifts the burden of proof to the IRS in any case regarding an item of income that was reconstructed by the IRS solely through the use of statistical data about unrelated taxpayers, including financial status audits. In cases of penalties, the IRS has the initial burden of proving the applicability of any penalty while the taxpayer has the burden of proving the applicability of any exception to the penalty.

EFFECTIVE DATE - Court proceedings arising in connection with examinations or taxable periods or events beginning or occurring after July 22, 1998.

INDIVIDUAL TEXT - p. 1-31.
COMPREHENSIVE TEXT - p. 1-31.

IRC § REFERENCE - §7491.

Innocent Spouse Relief

When a husband and wife file a joint return, they are jointly and severally liable for an tax deficiency for the year covered by the return. This means that the IRS can pursue either spouse for any tax delinquency it later uncovers. Often the IRS proceeds against whichever spouse is available (or solvent) regardless of who was responsible for the tax understatement. The law purports to alleviate the problem by exonerating the spouse who is innocent. Unfortunately innocent spouse relief is hard to come by and required the satisfaction of onerous conditions. One of these conditions required that the understatement was attributable to a "grossly erroneous" item.

As innocent spouse rules were at the center of recent allegations of IRS abuse, the Act makes innocent spouse relief easier to acquire. The Act eliminates all of the understatement thresholds and requires only that the understatement of tax be attributable to any erroneous, whether or not grossly erroneous, item of the other spouse.

A separate liability election for a taxpayer who, at the time of the election, is no longer married to, is legally separated from, or has been living apart for at least 12 months from the person with whom the taxpayer filed an original return, is allowed. Such taxpayers may elect to have any tax deficiency limited to the portion of the deficiency that is attributable to the items allocable to the taxpayer. This election is not allowed if the IRS can demonstrate that assets were transferred between a married couple filing a joint return as part of a fraudulent scheme or if both spouses had actual knowledge of the understatement of the tax. This separate liability election must be made no later than two years after the IRS begins collection procedures against the innocent spouse seeking relief.

Finally, the Secretary of the Treasury can relieve an individual of any tax liability if relief is not available under the expanded innocent spouse rule or the separate liability election and it would be inequitable to hold such taxpayer liable for any unpaid tax or deficiency.

EFFECTIVE DATE - Applies to all tax liabilities arising after July 22, 1998 as well as any tax liability that is still unpaid as of July 22, 1998.

INDIVIDUAL TEXT - p. 4-20.
CODE & REGS - §§66 and 6015.

IRC § REFERENCE - §§66 and 6015.

Seizure of Principal Residence

No seizure of a principal residence of the taxpayer, the taxpayer's spouse, former spouse or minor child can occur without prior court approval. Notice of pending court action must be provided to the taxpayer and any relevant family member. At the court hearing, the IRS must demonstrate that the requirements of any applicable law or administrative procedure have been met, that the liability is owed, and that no reasonable alternative for the collection of the taxpayer's debt exists.

EFFECTIVE DATE - Collections commencing after January 18, 1999.

IRC § REFERENCE - §6334.

Offers-in-Compromise

The Act also extends the IRS's authority to accept offers-in-compromise. The IRS must develop and publish schedules of national and local allowances that will provide taxpayers entering into an offer-in-compromise with the adequate means of providing for basic living expenses. The IRS is required to consider the facts and circumstances of a particular taxpayer's case in determining whether the national and local schedules are adequate for that particular taxpayer. The IRS may not reject an offer-in-compromise from a low-income taxpayer solely on the basis of the amount of the offer.

The IRS may also not attempt to collect a levy while an offer-in-compromise is being processed, for 30 days after an offer-in-compromise has ben rejected, while any rejection of an offer-in-compromise is being appealed, and while an installment agreement is pending.

The Act finally requires that the IRS follow a generous policy in accepting offers-in-compromise to provide taxpayers an incentive for continuing to file tax returns and pay taxes.

EFFECTIVE DATE - Offers-in-compromise submitted after July 22, 1998 and levies pending after December 31, 1999.

CORPORATIONS TEXT - p. 16-13.
COMPREHENSIVE TEXT - p. 25-11.
ADVANCED TEXT - p. 14-15.

IRC § REFERENCE - §7122.

Taxpayer Proceedings

The Act provides taxpayers greatly increased rights to proceed against the IRS and its employees. Examples include:

1.   The hourly cap on attorney's fees is increased and the circumstances under which attorney's fees and administrative costs can be awarded to taxpayers is expanded.

2. A taxpayer can collect up to $100,000 in civil damages for actions of an officer or an employee of the IRS who negligently disregards provisions of the Code or the Regulations in the collection of any tax.

3. Civil damages of up to $1 million can be awarded a taxpayer for actions of an officer or an employee of the IRS who willfully violates provisions of the Bankruptcy Code relating to automatic stays.

4. Once any court has entered a judgment, the IRS is precluded from collecting any amount disallowed by the court and any amount paid in excess of the court's judgment is to be refunded to the taxpayer.

5. Civil action is also allowed in the case of a lien erroneously filed by the IRS. The owner of the property is required to apply to the Secretary of the Treasury for a certificate of discharge of property and to deposit cash or furnish a bond sufficient to protect the lien interest of the U.S.

EFFECTIVE DATE - Applies to cases commencing after July 22, 1998.

IRC § REFERENCE - §§7426(a), 7430(c), and 7433.

Other Protection for Taxpayers during Audit

The Act provides for uniform application of confidential privileged communication between the taxpayer and his practitioner. Prior to this Act, Federal tax law protected the confidentiality of communication between a taxpayer and his attorney but not with any nonattorney who was authorized to practice before the IRS, such as a CPA or an enrolled agent. The Act extends attorney-client privileged communication to such nonattorneys providing tax advice. All exceptions to the attorney-client privilege also apply to the nonattorney-client privilege.

New restrictions have also been placed on actual audit procedures. These include the following:

1. Limitation on the use of financial status audit techniques.

2. Protection of software trade secrets discovered during any audit.

3. Prohibitions of threats of audit to coerce certain agreements.

4. Taxpayer allowed to quash third-party summonses.

EFFECTIVE DATE - Generally, all IRS audits after July 22, 1998. Extension of privileged communication to nonattorneys applies to noncriminal tax matters before the IRS or as a part of any court action after July 22, 1998. Also applies to all communications made after July 22, 1998.

CORPORATIONS TEXT - pp. 16-8 through 16-10.
COMPREHENSIVE TEXT - pp. 25-6 through 25-9.
ADVANCED TEXT – pp. 14-8 through 14-12.

IRC § REFERENCE - §§7443, 7525, 7602, 7603, 7609, 7612, and 7613.

Other Protection for Taxpayers during Collection Activities

The Act specifies extensive formal procedures to insure due process where the IRS seeks to collect taxes by levy or seizure. These due process procedures also apply after notice of a Federal tax lien has been filed. Generally, the IRS must notify individual taxpayers of the filing of any Notice of Lien and to provide the taxpayer with a Notice of Intent to Levy. Neither notice will be effective for 30 days during which time the taxpayer may demand a hearing.

Additionally, the Act restrains certain collection activities carried on by the IRS. Applicable restrictions include the following:

1. Elimination of the extension of the statute of limitation on collections by agreement between the taxpayer and the IRS, except as part of an installment agreement.

2. Uniform and streamlined process for approving liens, levies, and seizures.

3. Modifications for certain levy exemption amounts.

4. Release of levy upon agreement that amount is uncollectible.

5. Levy prohibited during pendency of refund hearings.

6. Waiver of early withdrawal tax for IRS levies on employer-sponsored retirement plans or IRAs.

7. Prohibition of sales of seized property at less than minimum bid.

8. Uniform assets disposal mechanism.

EFFECTIVE DATE - Generally, all IRS collection activities after July 22, 1998.

CORPORATIONS TEXT - p. 16-7.
ADVANCED TEXT - pp. 14-8 through 14-12.

IRC § REFERENCE - §§6320 through 6343.

ENCOURAGEMENT OF ELECTRONIC FILING

The Act attempts to make great strides toward the creation of a "paperless" tax system and, accordingly, commits the IRS to establish a comprehensive strategy to encourage electronic filing. The stated goal is that at least 80 percent of all tax and information returns will be electronically filed by the year 2007. The Secretary of the Treasury is also required to implement a return-free tax system for appropriate individuals by the year 2008.

The Act takes few steps to actually implement electronic filing. However, it does extend the due date for filing information returns via electronic means from February 28 to March 31. It also allows that all computer-generated returns be electronically filed by the year 2002.

Otherwise, most of the Act's encouragement of electronic filing is to require several reports, plans, and procedures. The Secretary of the Treasury is required to develop procedures that would eliminate the need to file a paper form relating to signature information. The Secretary of the Treasury must also develop a plan for receiving all forms electronically for taxable years after 1999. The Act also sets rules for determining when electronic returns are considered filed and for authorization for return preparers to communicate with the IRS on matters concerning electronically filed forms. The Secretary of the Treasury is also to devise a plan under which taxpayers can review their own accounts electronically by the year 2007, provided all necessary safeguards are in place by that date.

EFFECTIVE DATE - Various reports are due from January 18, 1999 through January 1, 2008.

IRC § REFERENCE - §§6071(b) and (c) and 6061.

OTHER PROVISIONS

The new law makes numerous miscellaneous provisions. Examples of interest include the following:

1.   The IRS Commissioner must report on problems and resolution of any Year 2000 computing problems.

2.   The IRS Commissioner must study and report on the future status of the current payment program for informants.

3.   The IRS can fund, on a matching basis, low-income taxpayer clinics.

4.   Written determination made by the IRS Chief Legal Counsel must be disclosed.

5.   The IRS must publish the telephone number of its nearest office in every telephone directory in the U.S.

6.   All tax payments must be made payable to "U.S. Treasury" not "IRS."

EFFECTIVE DATE - Generally, July 22, 1998.

PART 2: OTHER TAX PROVISIONS IN THE ACT

PROVISIONS RELATING TO CAPITAL GAINS

One-Year Holding Period for Long - Term Capital Gains

For sales of capital assets after 1997, the required holding period for determining long-term capital gains and losses is reduced from greater than 18 months to greater than 12 months. Property that qualifies for the shorter holding period includes property that qualifies for the normal 20 percent rate (or 10 percent in the case of 15 percent bracket taxpayers) and the 25 percent rate on certain real property gains, and the 28 percent rate on uncollectables and §1202 gain.

EFFECTIVE DATE - Property dispositions after December 31, 1997.

INDIVIDUAL TEXT - pp. 3-27 through 3-29 and Chapter 16.

CORPORATIONS TEXT - pp. 2-11 and 2-12.
COMPREHENSIVE TEXT - pp. 2-28 and 2-29 and Chapter 13.
BUSINESS ENTITIES TEXT - Chapter 8.
CODE & REGS - §1.

IRC § REFERENCE -§1(h).

NOTE: As mentioned in the introduction to this supplement, changes in capital gain and loss treatment are only highlighted here. Pages 3-27 through 3-29 of Chapter 3 of the INDIVIDUAL TEXT and all of Chapter 16 of the INDIVIDUAL TEXT have been rewritten. Both are currently available on the WEST/South-Western College Publishing website at tax.swcollege.com. Go there now.

Capital Gains and Losses Netting Rules

Among the more glaring errors of the Taxpayer Relief Act of 1997 was the omission of rules for netting an individual taxpayer's capital gains and losses. This netting process was mandated by the new 20 percent and 25 percent rates on long-term capital gains. The new rules generally provide that capital gains and losses are first netted in each category. A net capital loss within a category is offset against the highest taxed gain first (e.g., a net short-term capital loss is offset against capital gains taxed at the 28 percent maximum rate, then against capital gains taxed at the 25 percent rate, and finally against capital gains taxed at the 20 percent rate [or the 10 percent rate in the case of taxpayers in the 15 percent bracket]).

EFFECTIVE DATE - Property dispositions after May 6, 1997.

INDIVIDUAL TEXT - pp. 3-27 through 3-29 and Chapter 16.
CORPORATIONS TEXT - pp. 2-11 and 2-12.
COMPREHENSIVE TEXT - pp. 2-28 and 2-29 and Chapter 13.
BUSINESS ENTITIES TEXT - Chapter 8.
CODE & REGS - §1.

IRC § REFERENCE - §1(h).

NOTE: As mentioned in the introduction to this supplement, changes in capital gain and loss treatment are only highlighted here. Pages 3-27 through 3-29 of Chapter 3 of the INDIVIDUAL TEXT and all of Chapter 16 of the INDIVIDUAL TEXT have been rewritten. Both are currently available on the WEST/South-Western College Publishing website at tax.swcollege.com. Go there now.

PROVISIONS RELATING TO DEFERRED COMPENSATION

Deduction for Deferred Compensation

Compensation will no longer be considered as paid or received until it is actually received by the employee. Therefore, all types of compensation will not be deductible in the year accrued unless actual payment is made to the employee. This provision is a partial reversal of the Tax Court's 1996 ruling in *Schmidt Baking Co., Inc. v. Comm'r*. The Tax Court there ruled that vacation and severance pay were not deferred compensation but could still be deducted by an accrual method taxpayer in the year of the accrual.

The new law also provides that taxpayers required to change their accounting methods due to this provision must make all adjustments required by this change equally over a three-year period beginning with the first tax year covered under this provision.

EFFECTIVE DATE - Taxable years ending after July 22, 1998.

INDIVIDUAL TEXT - pp. 19-30 and 19-31.
ADVANCED TEXT - pp. 7-30 and 7-31.

IRC § REFERENCE - §404(a)(11).

Income Recognition on Rollovers into Roth IRAs

Traditional IRAs can be converted into Roth IRAs provided that the full amount of the traditional deductible IRA account and earnings for a nondeductible IRA account converted are included in gross income. Under prior law, if this conversion occurs before 1999, the income resulting from the conversion must be recognized ratably over a four-year period beginning in the year of the conversion. The new law permits the taxpayer new options. The taxpayer may recognize the income ratably over the four-year period or may include the entire amount in the current year.

Example: Barbara converts traditional deductible IRA accounts totalling $100,000 into several Roth IRA accounts on July 1, 1998. Under prior law, she would have been required to include in gross income $25,000 for each of the years 1998, 1999, 2000, and 2001. Under the new law, she can elect the old law treatment or she can elect to include in gross income the full

$100,000 amount in 1998.

Care must be exercised in that any election to use the four-year rule cannot be changed after the due date for filing a tax return for that year. For example, if Barbara in the above example elected to use the four-year rule and included in gross income $25,000 in 1998, her election could not be changed after the due date for filing her 1998 return, normally April 15, 1999.

If the four-year period is chosen, certain restrictions apply. Whenever a portion of the converted amount is withdrawn before it is recognized as income, the withdrawn amount must be recognized as income during the year of the withdrawal. In no case, can the taxpayer recognize as income an amount greater than the withdrawal. If the taxpayer owning the Roth IRA account dies before the end of the four-year period, all untaxed amounts shall be included in the gross income of the taxpayer for the year of death, unless any such untaxed income is inherited by a surviving spouse. In this case, the surviving spouse can elect to recognize any untaxed amounts over the four-year period elected by the deceased taxpayer. This election is also irrevocable after the due date for the decedent's last tax return.

EFFECTIVE DATE - Taxable years beginning after December 31, 1997.

INDIVIDUAL TEXT - p. 19-29.
ADVANCED TEXT - pp. 7-28 and 7-29.
CODE & REGS - §408A.

IRC § REFERENCE - §408A(d)(3).

AGI Limit on Rollovers into Roth IRAs: Income Effect

Traditional IRAs can be converted into Roth IRAs if the AGI of the taxpayer does not exceed $100,000. The new law provides that amounts included in gross income as the result of the IRA conversion are not to be included in applying the AGI ceiling.

EFFECTIVE DATE - Taxable years beginning after December 31, 1997.

INDIVIDUAL TEXT - p. 19-29.
ADVANCED TEXT - pp. 7-28 and 7-29.
CODE & REGS - §408A.

IRC § REFERENCE - §408A(c)(3)(C)(i).

AGI Limit on Rollovers into Roth IRAs: Age 70 1/2

Traditional IRAs can be converted into Roth IRAs if the AGI of the taxpayer does not exceed $100,000. The new law provides that the actual calculation of the AGI limit does not include required minimum distributions from IRAs for individuals who are at least 70 1/2 years of age. Any required minimum distribution remains ineligible for conversion and must be included in gross income.

EFFECTIVE DATE - Taxable years beginning after December 31, 2004.

INDIVIDUAL TEXT - p. 19-29.
ADVANCED TEXT - pp. 7-28 and 7-29.
CODE & REGS - §408A.

IRC § REFERENCE - §408A(c)(3)(C)(i).

Education IRAs

The Act makes several critical clarifications regarding an education IRA. All distributions from an education IRA account will be treated as a ratable share of the principle and accumulated earnings in the account. If an excess contribution remains in the account, an excise tax of 10 percent will be levied. The entire balance of the education IRA account will be treated as being distributed and taxed within 30 days after the beneficiary either reaches 30 years of age or dies. The account may also be rolled over tax free into another education IRA upon the death of the beneficiary or the beneficiary attaining age 30. The new beneficiary may be any member of the former beneficiary's family under the age of 30.

EFFECTIVE DATE - Taxable years beginning after December 31, 1997.
INDIVIDUAL TEXT - p. 19-24.
ADVANCED TEXT - p. 7-23.
CODE & REGS - §530.

IRC § REFERENCE - §§530(b) and (d).

SIMPLE Plans in Cases of Acquisitions and Dispositions

An employer who fails to continue to meet the eligibility requirements of a SIMPLE plan by reason of an acquisition, disposition, or similar transaction is still treated as meeting the requirements if coverage under the plan is not significantly changed. In this case, the SIMPLE plan may be maintained as a qualified salary reduction plan after the transaction for a grace period. The grace period begins on the date of the transaction and ends on the last day of the second calendar year in which the transaction occurs. For such treatment, the employer must remain a qualified employer, the employer must have only one plan, and all other participation requirements must be satisfied.

EFFECTIVE DATE - Taxable years beginning after December 31, 1996.

INDIVIDUAL TEXT - p. 19-19.
ADVANCED TEXT - pp. 7-18 and 7-19.

IRC § REFERENCE - §408(p)(10).

PROVISIONS REGARDING SALE OF PRINCIPAL RESIDENCE

Exclusion of Gain on Sale of Principal Residence
by Married Couples

Under §121, the amount of excludible gain on the sale of a principal residence may be doubled from $250,000 to $500,000 in the case of married couples filing joint returns. This section requires the following: (1) either spouse must have owned the house for two of the past five years, (2) both spouses must have used the property as a principal place of residence for at least two of the past five years, and (3) neither spouse has excluded gain on a the sale of a principal residence over the past two years. The new law retains all of these provisions, but clarifies the treatment of married couples where one spouse fails to meet any of the three restrictions. In such a case, the $250,000 limitation shall apply to each spouse individually as if the couple were not married. Additionally, each spouse is to be treated as owning the property during the two year period that either spouse owned the property.
Example: John and Janet were married on June 3, 1997 at which time Janet moved into John's principal residence of the past 16 years. Janet sold her old home on December 3, 1996 and claimed the §121 exclusion for that year. On August 9, 1998, John's house is sold for a realized gain of $440,000. They file a joint return for 1998. Since Janet fails the second and third tests, she cannot qualify for the exclusion. But John still qualifies for the $250,000 exclusion so that their recognized gain is $190,000 ($440,000 - $250,000).

EFFECTIVE DATE - Sales of residences after May 6, 1997.

INDIVIDUAL TEXT - pp. 15-18 and 15-19.
COMPREHENSIVE TEXT - pp. 12-41 and 12-42.

BUSINESS ENTITIES TEXT - p. 7-34.
ADVANCED TEXT - p. 8-24.
CODE & REGS - §121.

IRC § REFERENCE - §121(b)(2).

Exclusion of Gain on Sale of Principal Residence under Relief Provision

As stated above, the amount of excludible gain on the sale of a principal residence is doubled from $250,000 to $500,000 in the case of certain married couples filing joint returns. Taxpayers who fail to own and use the house as the principal residence for at least two out of the past five years or who fail the two years between sales test can still exclude a portion of their gain if they meet the relief provision of §121(c)(2)(B).

The new law, however, provides that the exclusion is determined as a fraction of the maximum exclusion ($250,000 or $500,000 for married couples) rather than as a fraction of the realized gain. The calculation of the fraction of the maximum exclusion remains the same as under prior law. The numerator is the number of qualifying months and the denominator is 24 months.

Example: Clare, a single taxpayer, owned and lived in a principal residence in St. Louis for 12 months before being transferred to Houston in December, 1998. Her realized gain on the sale is $300,000. Since she qualifies for the relief provision, she can exclude $125,000 (12 months / 24 months X $250,000). Her recognized gain is $175,000 ($300,000 - $125,000).

EFFECTIVE DATE - Sales of residences after May 6, 1997.

INDIVIDUAL TEXT - pp. 15-19 and 15-20.
COMPREHENSIVE TEXT - p. 12-42.
CODE & REGS - §121.

IRC § REFERENCE - §121(c)(1)
PROVISIONS AFFECTING CORPORATE OWNERSHIP

Special Rules for Distributions to Shareholders

The Act clarifies that in determining control under §351, the fact that any corporate transferor distributes part or all of the stock which it receives in the exchange is considered irrelevant. The same result would hold in a similar transaction satisfying the requirements of §355. In addition, in a tax free corporate reorganization, the shareholders of the distributing corporation may dispose of part or all of their stock. These provisions clarify the issue of stock distributed immediately after a tax-free transaction.

EFFECTIVE DATE - Transfers after August 5, 1997.

CORPORATIONS TEXT - pp. 3-6 and 5-19.
COMPREHENSIVE TEXT - p. 17-6.
BUSINESS ENTITIES TEXT – pp. 9-11 and 9-12.

IRC § REFERENCE - §§351(c) and 368(a)(2)(H)(ii).

Nonqualified Preferred Stock in §351 Transactions

The receipt of nonqualified preferred stock does not qualify for nonrecognition of gain under §351. Under the old rules, the fair market value of the stock would have been treated as boot. Under the new rules, nonqualified preferred stock will trigger gain, but not loss, if, and only if, the transferor receives stock other than nonqualified preferred stock. If only nonqualified preferred stock is received, the taxpayer is treated as having sold the transferred property to the corporation. As a result, gain or loss may be recognized.

EFFECTIVE DATE - Transfers after June 8, 1997.

CORPORATIONS TEXT - p. 3-5.
COMPREHENSIVE TEXT - p. 17-5.

IRC § REFERENCE - §351(g)(1)(B).

Foreign Corporations Involved in §304 Transactions

Under the general rule of §304, whenever a taxpayer transfers stock of a corporation within a controlled group to another corporation in the group, the exchange is considered as a redemption of stock of the acquiring corporation. The new rules instruct the Secretary of the Treasury to set new regulations whenever either the acquiring or issuing corporation is a foreign corporation. The intent behind the Regulations is to prohibit a multiple inclusion of income and to provide for the appropriate adjustment of the bases of all stock involved. Double taxation and unreasonable bases reductions were possible under prior law due to the constructive dividend approach of the controlled foreign corporation regime and the application of §§959 and 961.

EFFECTIVE DATE - Distributions and acquisitions after June 8, 1997.

CORPORATIONS TEXT - pp. 5-18 and 9-30.
ADVANCED TEXT - pp. 1-18 and 5-32.

IRC § REFERENCE - §304(b)(6).

§1045 Treatment for Nonindividual Taxpayers

Section 1045 provides that the recognition of gain on the sale of qualified small business stock as defined in §1044 can be avoided if the proceeds are used to buy stock in another similar corporation within 60 days. Under prior law, this treatment was limited to individual shareholders. Under the Act, any shareholder other than a corporation is eligible for nonrecognition of gain under §1045. Thus, partnerships, trusts, and estates can avoid recognition of gain on the sale of a qualified small business stock.

EFFECTIVE DATE - Sales of qualifying stock after August 5, 1997.

INDIVIDUAL TEXT - p. 15-22.
COMPREHENSIVE TEXT - p. 12-45.
BUSINESS ENTITIES TEXT - p. 8-23.
CODE & REGS - §1045.

IRC § REFERENCE - §1045(a).

OTHER BUSINESS PROVISIONS

Deductibility of Employer Provided Meals

The new law expands §119 coverage on employer-provided meals. This section provides that the value of meals provided to employees on the business premises of the employer for the convenience of the employer are deductible by the employer and excludible by the employee. Under prior law, where some employer-provided meals were provided for the convenience of the employer and others were not for the convenience of the employer, the determination had to be made on an employee-by-employee basis.

The new law removes this burdensome requirement. All meals provided to employees on the employer's business premises are to be treated as provided for the convenience of the employer if more than 50 percent of the employees receive meals for the employer's convenience. Thus, under §119, all such meals are deductible by the employer and excludible by the employees and the determination need not be made on an employee-by-employee basis.

EFFECTIVE DATE - Taxable years beginning before, on, or after July 22, 1998.

INDIVIDUAL TEXT - pp. 5-14 and 5-15.
COMPREHENSIVE TEXT - pp. 4-14 and 4-15.
BUSINESS ENTITIES TEXT - pp. 16-7 and 16-8.
CODE & REGS - §119.

IRC § REFERENCE - §119(b).

Small Business AMT Exemption

The Act clarifies two issues regarding the small business exemption under corporate AMT rules. First, in applying the $7.5 million average gross receipt test, only taxable years beginning after December 31, 1993 are considered. Secondly, all corporations are exempt from corporate AMT during their first year of existence regardless of income levels.

EFFECTIVE DATE - Taxable years beginning after December 31, 1997.

INDIVIDUAL TEXT - p. 12-28.
CORPORATIONS TEXT - p. 6-3.
COMPREHENSIVE TEXT - p. 14-28.
BUSINESS ENTITIES TEXT - p. 14-9.
CODE & REGS - §55.

IRC § REFERENCE - §55(e)(1).

Application of §732 to §751(c) Transactions

In treating the sales, exchanges or distributions of unrealized receivables as defined in §751(c), applicable provisions governing the basis of distributed property found in §732 apply.

EFFECTIVE DATE - Sales, exchanges and distributions after August 5, 1997.

CORPORATIONS TEXT - p. 11-25.
COMPREHENSIVE TEXT - p. 22-48
BUSINESS ENTITIES TEXT - p. 14-28.

ADVANCED TEXT - pp. 4-24 and 25.

IRC § REFERENCE - §§732 and 751(c).

OTHER PROVISIONS

Student Loan Interest

The new law provides that only a taxpayer who is required to make interest payments on a qualified education loan under the terms of the loan may deduct such payments as student loan interest.

EFFECTIVE DATE - Taxable years beginning after December 31, 1997.

INDIVIDUAL TEXT - p. 10-13.
COMPREHENSIVE TEXT - p. 15-44.
CODE & REGS - §221.

IRC § REFERENCE - §221(e)(1).

Qualified State Tuition Programs

The beneficiary's spouse is now included in the definition of a family member with respect to rollovers and beneficiary designation changes under a qualified state tuition program.

EFFECTIVE DATE - Taxable years beginning after August 20, 1996.

INDIVIDUAL TEXT - p. 5-29.
CODE & REGS - §529.

IRC § REFERENCE - §529(e)(2).

APPENDIX

West's Internal Revenue Code of 1986 and
Treasury Regulations: Annotated and Selected

[Note: Page references are to the pages of this supplement where the coverage appears.]